# A New True Book

# MONKEYS AND APES

### By Kathryn Wentzel Lumley

This "true book" was prepared
under the direction of
Illa Podendorf,
formerly with the Laboratory School,
University of Chicago

CHILDRENS PRESS ™

CHICAGO

Capuchin monkey

PHOTO CREDITS

Zoological Society of San Diego—2, 10 (lower left), 21 (D.K. Brockman), 22 (bottom), 27, 37 (2 photos)

Allan Roberts—4, 10 (lower right), 19, 22 (top), 25, 39, (left), 40, 43

Root Resources: ©Kenneth W. Fink, Cover, 6, 16, 31; ©Anthony Mercieca—8

James P. Rowan—35 (2 photos), 39 (right), 44

Lynn M. Stone—10 (top), 15 (2 photos), 29

R.A. Masek—12

Ray Hillstrom—32, 41

Cover—Lowland gorilla

Library of Congress Cataloging in Publication Data

Lumley, Kathryn Wentzel.
  Monkeys and apes.

  (A New true book)
  Includes index.
  Summary: Describes the physical characteristics, habits, and natural environment of monkeys and apes.
  1.   Monkeys—Juvenile literature.
  2.   Apes—Juvenile literature. [1.   Apes.
  2.   Monkeys]   I.   Title.
  QL737.P9L85   1982         599.8        82-12779
  ISBN 0-516-01633-4           AACR2

# TABLE OF CONTENTS

One monkey is getting a drink; the other one is looking for peanuts.

# MONKEYS AND APES

Have you ever watched
monkeys and apes?
Sometimes they act like
people. They play and
have fun. They can use
their hands the way people
do. They peel bananas,
pick up food, and play ball.

Proboscis monkey. The word proboscis (pro • BOH • sis) is used to describe a very long or big nose, such as an elephant's trunk.

# OLD WORLD MONKEYS

Today monkeys who live
in Africa and Asia are
called Old World monkeys.
Some of them have tails,
but some do not. All Old
World monkeys have
nostrils very close together.

Old World monkeys have
names like colobus, langur,
baboon, and guenon. They

Baboon

are bigger and stronger
than New World monkeys.
Some Old World
monkeys live in trees.
Others live on the ground.

# NEW WORLD MONKEYS

The monkeys that live in South and Central America are called New World monkeys. Many of these monkeys have long tails. They can use their tails like a hand. The nostrils of New World monkeys are very far apart.

New World monkeys are small. The biggest weigh

Right: Woolly monkey
Below right: Cottontopped marmoset
Below left: Spider monkey

only about 15 to 20
pounds. All New World
monkeys live in trees.

If you hear about a
spider, a capuchin, a
woolly, a howler, or a night
monkey, you will know
they are New World
monkeys.

All monkeys are primates.

Chimpanzees

# APES

Apes are primates without tails. Apes are smarter than monkeys. The large ones are the great apes. Chimpanzees, orangutans, and gorillas are great apes.

Chimpanzees are very active. They like to play.

The orangutans and gorillas are very quiet. They do not move around very much. They are large and heavy.

Gorillas look fierce, but they are not fierce. They are called "the gentle giants of Africa." Sometimes male gorillas grow as tall as six feet and weigh 450 pounds.

Orangutan

Gorilla

White-cheeked gibbon

Gibbons are lesser apes. Gibbons never weigh more than 30 pounds. They live in trees. They use their long arms to swing from tree to tree. Some people call them tree walkers.

Apes live in the Old World. They can be found in Africa and Asia.

# HOW MONKEYS LIVE

The night monkeys sleep during the day. They look for food at night. Their bright eyes have white patches above them. They show up in the dark forests. A mother, father, and baby usually travel together. The father takes care of the baby except at feeding time.

Owl monkey
at night

Sometimes the night monkeys are called owl monkeys.

The howler monkeys are the largest of the New World monkeys.

Howler monkeys have "howling times." A male monkey begins making a noise. Then all the others who are around join in. They begin about five o'clock in the morning and howl for about an hour. Other troops of howler monkeys answer them.

Red Howler monkeys

This helps the monkeys
stay out of each other's
way while looking for food.
The tails of these monkeys
have prints on the
underside just like
fingerprints. Their tails are
very strong.

Above: Squirrel
monkey
Right: Black-handed
spider monkey

22

The squirrel monkeys are tiny. They weigh only two or three pounds. Their tails cannot be used for swinging in the trees.

Spider monkeys spend most of their time up in the trees. They are big monkeys. Their tails are longer than their bodies. Some of them weigh 15 pounds.

The spider monkeys are fast. They almost seem to fly across the tops of the trees. Their tails are strong. Their tails can hold all of their weight. If they are scared, they break off branches and throw them. They can also make barking noises.

The woolly monkeys have short thick fur on their heads. That is how they got their name. They

South American
woolly monkey

hunt on the ground and in the trees. They can walk on two legs if they use their arms to keep their balance. Sometimes they sit down and use their strong tails to hold them up.

Only the howler monkeys are larger than the woollies.

The capuchin monkeys spend a lot of time on the ground. They are smart. They can use sticks to get food they can't reach. They open nuts by hitting them against something hard. The capuchin monkeys are the organ-grinders' monkeys. They are small, easy to train, and can put on a good show.

Capuchin

27

The baboons are able to live on the ground or in the trees. Many of them are fierce. They will fight other animals.

Some monkeys travel in groups. These groups are called troops. A troop has a male monkey as a leader. The troop always includes females and their babies. There could be other males in the group, too.

Baboons

They live and travel
together to look for food.
They eat insects, leaves,
small birds, birds' eggs,
and fruit. When they find
plenty of food they stay
awhile.

29

# HOW APES LIVE

Chimpanzees like to live in large groups of 70 or 80. They form small groups or troops to look for food.

Gorillas live in troops. They like to be together. A big male is the leader. He is always one of the oldest males.

Male, lowland gorilla

Monkeys and apes that live on the ground need a strong leader. The leader works hard to keep his troop safe.

The troop travels through the forest looking for food. They spend six or eight hours a day looking for food and eating it.

They eat leaves, insects, eggs, and vines. Some apes even eat meat. But gorillas and orangutans

Chimpanzee

usually eat vegetables and fruits.

If anything scares a gorilla troop, the leader puts on a show. He growls and hoots. Then he cups his hand and beats his chest. It makes a loud empty sound.

After making these sounds for awhile the leader hits the ground to make even more noise. Then he runs through the forest and slaps at the bushes. He jumps up and down. He wants to scare away the enemy, not fight.

The other males help the leader make noises. Even the baby apes beat on their chests and scream. They also slap their little bellies or hit another ape. They want to help save the troop.

Five-month-old gorilla

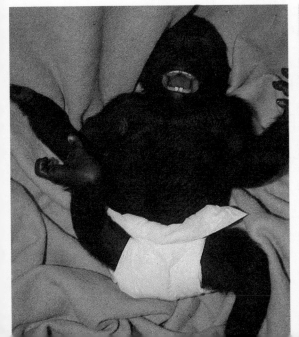

Baby orangutan

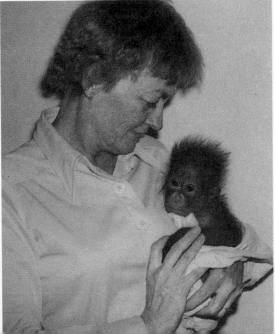

# BABY MONKEYS AND APES

Monkeys and apes are good parents. They help their babies grow up.

The mother monkeys and apes nurse their babies. The babies drink their mothers' milk.

Above: Capuchin monkeys and baby
Left: Pigmy chimpanzee and baby

The mothers take very
good care of their babies.
They keep them warm and
safe. When the babies are
tiny, they stay with their
parents all the time.

The young have many things to learn. They need to know which plants are good to eat and how to find water. They must learn their place in the troop. They must know what the sounds made by the grown-ups mean. Some sounds tell them that danger is near. If they know these sounds, it can save them from getting hurt. They learn all these things from their mothers.

Left: Golden lion marmoset
Above: South American titi monkey

# SOME THINGS
# TO REMEMBER

New World monkeys are
smaller than Old World
monkeys. Apes are the
largest and strongest of all.

Long-tailed
macque

New World monkeys
have nostrils that are far
apart and face sideways.

Old World monkeys have
nostrils that are close
together. They face
downward and outward.

40

New World monkeys cannot use their thumbs to pick up things.

Old World monkeys have thumbs that can be used opposite another finger to pick things up. This is called "opposable."

Can you see the thumb on this monkey?

New World monkeys
often have strong tails that
can wrap around things.
They are prehensile tails.
Old World monkeys
never have prehensile tails.
Apes have no tails.
New World monkeys live
in trees. They are usually
smaller than Old World
monkeys.
There are many more
interesting and exciting

Rhesus monkey

things to find out about
monkeys and apes. There
is always something new
to learn. Many people
study them. They go to the
forests where the monkeys
and apes live. They watch
them to find out about

Siamangs are the largest gibbons.

them. You can read more books about the things monkeys and apes do. You can go to the zoo to watch them.

When someone tells you that you are "monkeying around," you will know that they mean you are having fun!

# WORDS YOU SHOULD KNOW

**balance**(BAL • ence) — to be in a steady position

**fierce**(FEERSS) — dangerous

**nostril**(NAHSS • trill) — one of the outer openings of the nose

**nurse**(NERSE) — to feed a young animal at a milk gland on the mother animal

**opposable thumb**(op • OZE • uh • bil) — a thumb that can be used with another finger to hold things

**prehensile tail**(pree • HEN • sil) — a part of an animal's body that can be wrapped around an object

**primate**(PRY • mait) — a mammal animal group that includes human beings, monkeys, and apes

**props**(PROPSS) — something used to keep another thing in position; a support

**sac**(SACK) — a baglike structure hanging from an animal's body

# INDEX

About the Author:

Mrs. Lumley is a nationally known reading specialist and author of numerous books and articles on reading and its teaching. Her experience includes teaching at all levels from elementary through university classes, and director of the Reading Center for the Washington, D.C. Public Schools. Mrs. Lumley is a member of the board of directors of Reading is Fundamental (RIF). She is also a Trustee of the Williamsport (Pa.) Area Community College and is an active participant in leading professional associations.

# A New True Book

# EARTHQUAKES

**By Helen J. Challand, Ph. D.**

This "true book" was prepared
under the direction of
Illa Podendorf,
formerly with the Laboratory School,
University of Chicago

CHILDRENS PRESS, CHICAGO

An earthquake caused the land in
the foreground of this picture to sink
ten feet.

Library of Congress Cataloging in Publication Data

Challand, Helen J.
Earthquakes.

(A New true book)
Includes index.
Summary: Briefly describes the earth's interior,
the forces and stresses that sometimes cause the
ground to shake, and the effects of such movement.
1. Earthquakes—Juvenile literature. [1. Earth-
quakes] I. Title.
QE521.3.C45  1982        551.2'2      82-9699
ISBN 0-516-01636-9          AACR2

# TABLE OF CONTENTS

# WHAT DOES THE EARTH LOOK LIKE?

The earth is a ball of rocks. It is almost round. Water and land are on top of these rocks.

The large areas of water are called lakes and oceans. The smaller ones are ponds, marshes, and swamps. Long flowing waters are called streams and rivers.

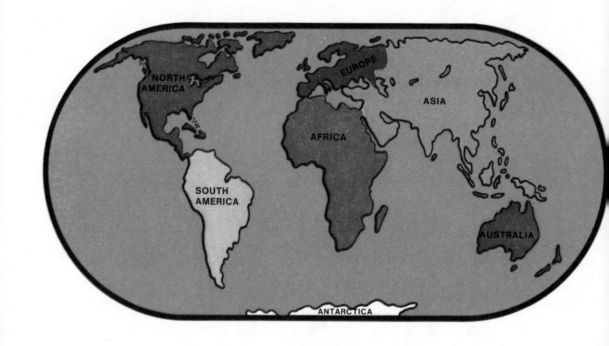

The large land areas are the continents. Today there are seven continents. They are North America, South America, Europe, Asia, Africa, Australia, and Antarctica.

# WHAT DID THE EARTH LOOK LIKE LONG AGO?

Two hundred million years ago there was only one large mass of land. The rest of the earth was covered with water.

Slowly this one landmass broke up into smaller pieces. These hunks of land moved only a few inches or feet each year.

# WHAT DOES
# THE EARTH LOOK LIKE
# ON THE INSIDE?

The inside of the earth has three parts.

The center is called the core. It is about 3,200 miles thick. The core is made of iron and nickel. It is solid and very hot.

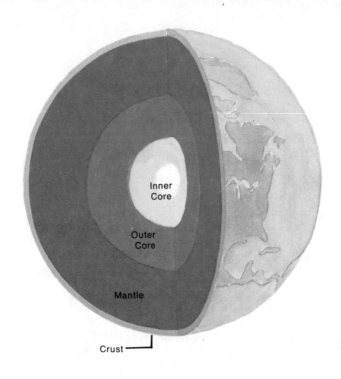

Inner
Core

Outer
Core

Mantle

Crust

The outer part of the
core is almost a liquid.
Around the core is
another layer called the
mantle. It is about 1,800
miles thick.

Most of the mantle is made of solid rock. Iron, magnesium, and silicon are found in this rock. A thin layer on the outside of the mantle is very hot. Here the rocks form a thick liquid.

The crust is the outer layer of the earth. It is 0 to 30 miles thick.

In the land areas the crust is usually granite.

Granite mountains

Under the ocean the
rocks are made of basalt.
Plants, animals, and
people live on and in the
earth's crust.

After the earthquake in Alaska, 1964

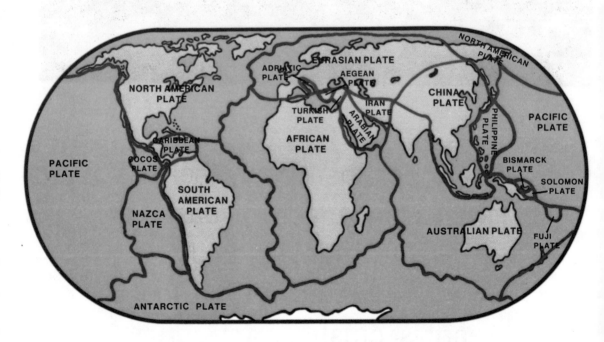

The plates fit together like the pieces of a jigsaw puzzle.

# WHAT CAUSES EARTHQUAKES?

Scientists believe that the earth's crust is made of 8 to 12 huge pieces called plates. These plates are made of rock.

These plates are always moving.

The earth is very restless. As the plates move, rocks slide, crack, sink, and groan. Sometimes a huge rock gets caught against another one. The pressure builds up.

Rocks can be stretched and pushed out of shape. They may not move for years. Pressure builds. A great deal of energy is stored. Finally, the rocks can stand no more pressure. They shake and crumble and cause an earthquake.

An earthquake causes
the air to move. It sounds
like thunder.
Land rises and falls.

Mountains can be split
in half. Hills and bluffs
tumble down. Huge ice
blocks slide down the
sides of mountains.

The cement on the
highways rises up into
large hills. Railroad tracks
twist and buckle.

Cars fall into big holes
in the ground.

Workers cleaning up earthquake damage in California

Buildings tremble and break.

Water and sewer pipes crack open. Power lines and telephone lines fall down.

Often there are fires after a big earthquake.

# HOW LONG DOES AN EARTHQUAKE LAST?

An earthquake usually lasts only a few seconds. Some big ones have lasted five minutes. The little tremors or twitches can be felt for days.

Earthquake damage in the village of Santorini (san • tor • EE • nee)

# HOW MANY AND
# HOW BAD ARE THEY?

There are several thousand earthquakes each year. Only about 100 of them are bad.

China has had the worst earthquake so far. In 1556 it shook the earth so hard that 830,000 people were killed.

Earthquake damage in Skoplje (SKOP • la), Yugoslavia (yoo • go • SLAH • via)

A bad earthquake can release as much energy as 2,000 atomic bombs exploding.

# HOW STRONG IS AN EARTHQUAKE?

Scientists use an instrument to record the strength of a quake. It is called a seismograph. It

Above: Cross-sectioned seismometer, an instrument used to measure conditions in the earth. Right: Seismic recorder used to measure aftershocks.

can pick up shock waves as far as 600 miles away.

The waves are measured on a Richter scale. This scale goes from 1 to 9.

A reading of 2 is 30 times stronger than a reading of 1.

If an earthquake measures below 4 on the scale, it usually does not do much damage. When it goes over 7 it causes destruction.

# WHAT IS A FAULT?

A fault is a crack in the crust of the earth. It is a scar left by old earthquakes.

A famous fault in California is called the San Andreas Fault. It looks like a valley. It is 600 miles long and is millions of years old.

1906 San
Francisco
earthquake

A big quake happened
along this fault on April 18,
1906. The ground moved
over ten feet in some
places. It caused the
famous San Francisco fire.

California has over 100
earthquakes each year.
Most of them are small.

The last big one was near San Fernando in 1971. It killed over sixty people.

It did millions of dollars worth of damage to homes and stores. It added four feet to the height of the San Gabriel Mountains.

# SAN ANDREAS FAULT

The floating plates that cover the earth are slowly moving. The San Andreas Fault is the line between two plates.

Los Angeles is on a different plate than San Francisco. Los Angeles is on a plate moving north.

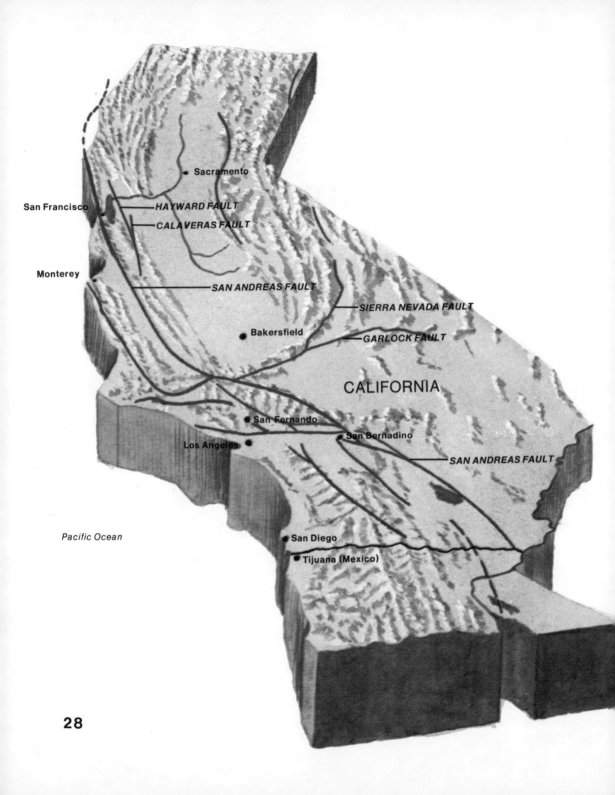

San Francisco

Sacramento

*HAYWARD FAULT*

*CALAVERAS FAULT*

Monterey

*SAN ANDREAS FAULT*

*SIERRA NEVADA FAULT*

Bakersfield

*GARLOCK FAULT*

CALIFORNIA

San Fernando

San Bernadino

Los Angeles

*SAN ANDREAS FAULT*

Pacific Ocean

San Diego

Tijuana (Mexico)

28

San Francisco is on a plate with the rest of the United States. This floating rocky plate is slowly moving south.

Millions of years ago the part of California west of the fault was much farther south. It was once where Mexico is today.

Millions of years from now Los Angeles and San Francisco will be next to each other.

Parícutin (pah • REE • ka • teen) Volcano
erupted in 1943.

# EARTHQUAKES
# AND VOLCANOES

Earthquakes do not
always make volcanoes.
But volcanoes can make
the earth quake.

A volcano is active when a spot in the earth opens up. Steam, hot gases, and liquid rock spill out. This liquid rock is called lava. It is called magma when it is still inside the ground.

Hawaii is a chain of islands formed by lava.

Lava flow from a 1973 eruption of Mauna Ulu (MAW • nah OO • loo) Crater on the slopes of Kileuea (kee • LOH • ay • ah) Volcano

In 1943 an earthquake in Mexico caused a volcano to form. It started in the middle of a farmer's field. It grew 1,200 feet high in ten years.

Several new islands in Iceland were formed by volcanoes.

Mount St. Helens erupted in 1980

# THE RING OF FIRE

Earthquakes are common around the edge of the Pacific Ocean. This rim is called the ring of fire. Many volcanoes are found here. They are caused by earthquakes.

North and South America have earthquakes. They happen in Italy, Greece, India, Iran, and Algeria, too.

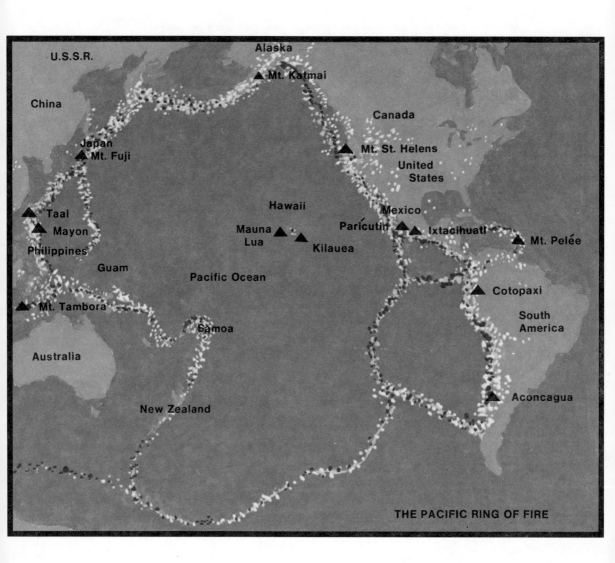

THE PACIFIC RING OF FIRE

On the other side of the Pacific Ocean the ring of fire continues. There are earthquakes in the Philippines, Japan, China, and the Aleutian Islands.

One earthquake in Alaska broke a record. It happened on March 27, 1964. It measured almost 9 on the Richter scale. The ground rose fifty feet. This is higher than most school buildings.

# EARTHQUAKES
# UNDER THE WATER

Earthquakes can happen under the sea. They can raise or lower the ocean floor.

An earthquake in Chile caused a tidal wave that caused this damage in Hilo, Hawaii 6,800 miles away.

Earthquakes can cause huge landslides under the water. This makes waves. The waves circle out in all directions. They stop when they hit something such as the shore of a continent. These waves have a special name. They are called tsunamis.

After an earthquake these waves may travel for hundreds of miles. They can move at 600 miles an hour. By the time the waves reach a shore they may be 100 feet high. A huge wall of water pours onto the land.

An earthquake in the Gulf of Alaska caused big waves to hit Hawaii. Once a whole city was drowned.

Tidal wave damage on Hawaii

# CAN PEOPLE
# SHAKE THE EARTH ?

Yes, people have caused earthquakes. This happens when water or wastes are pumped into deep wells. This puts a lot of pressure on and in the rock layers. If it is too great, the rocks will move suddenly. This causes an earthquake.

# CAN SOMETHING BE DONE ABOUT EARTHQUAKES?

Scientists believe that someday a safe way can be found to stop the earth from shaking.

Laser ranging instrument used to measure earth changes along a fault line. Over 10,000 earthquakes have been recorded by scientists.

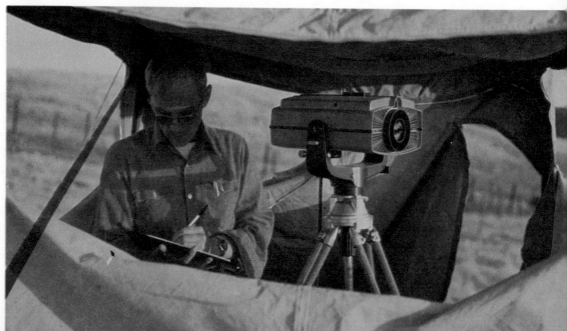

Some kind of liquid could be pumped into faults. This would be like oiling the rocks. The floating plates of rocks would then slide by each other. This would keep them from getting stuck and breaking loose.

Scientist are developing instruments that can measure the slightest tremble. They can even record the creeping along of rocks.

In earthquake areas buildings must be able to withstand shaking. They should be made of steel frames. Concrete walls need metal rods running through them.

During an earthquake wooden houses can bend and sway more than brick ones.

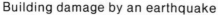
Building damage by an earthquake

# MYTHS ABOUT EARTHQUAKES

Today we know what causes earthquakes. But once upon a time people had many wild ideas about what caused them.

Some thought the earth was riding on the back of a giant turtle. When the turtle moved, parts of the earth would crack.

Others thought we were riding a huge frog.

The strangest idea was that the earth was on the head of a bull. People thought there were four bulls. An earthquake was caused when one bull tossed the earth to another bull.

An earthquake caused part of this bridge to collapse.

This damage to Anchorage, Alaska was caused by a 1964 earthquake.

We know now these
stories were all myths.
Scientist today know why
the earth snaps, crackles,
and pops.

# WORDS YOU SHOULD KNOW

**area**(AIR • ee • ah) — a section or region.

**basalt**(bah • SAWLT) — a type of rock formed from lava.

**buckle**(BUK • ihl) — to bend or twist.

**continent**(KAHN • tin • ent) — one of the seven main landmasses of the earth.

**core**(KOR) — the center of the earth.

**crust**(KRUSST) — the outer layer of the earth surrounding the mantle.

**damage**(DAM • ij) — to do harm; to destroy.

**destruction**(deh • STRUK • shun) — damage or serious harm.

**earthquakes**(irth • KWAKES) — a shaking of the ground caused by sudden movements of rocks underneath the earth's surface.

**energy**(EN • er • gee) — power to do work.

**fault**(FAWLT) — a crack in the crust of the earth.

**granite**(GRAN • it) — a kind of rock that is formed from lava.

**huge**(HYOOJ) — very big.

**hunk** — piece.

**landslide**(LAND • slyde) — the sliding down of a part of the land.

**lava**(LAH • vah) — hot, melted rock that flows from a volcano.

**magma**(MAG • mah) — melted rock under the earth's surface.

**magnesium**(mag • NEE • zee • um) — a metal that is light and fairly hard.

**mantle**(MAN • till) — the layer of the earth around the core and below the crust.

**mass** — a large amount or piece.

**myth**(MITH) — a story that is not true.

**plate**(PLAYT) — part of the crust of the earth.

**predict**(prih • DIKT) — to tell what will happen before it happens.

**pressure**(PRESH • ur) — to put force on something; to push.

**San Andreas**(SAN an • DRAY • us) **Fault**—the name of a fault in
    California.

**seismic**(SIZE • mik)—of or relating to earthquakes.

**seismograph**(SIZE • me • graf)—an instrument that measures the
    force of an earthquake.

**seisometer**(size • OM • iter)—instrument used to measure earth
    movement.

**sewer** (SOO • er)—a pipe that carries waste water.

**silicon** (SILL • ih • kahn)—an element found in many of the rocks
    and minerals of the earth.

**tremble** (TREM • bil)—to shake.

**tremor**(TREM • er)—a shaking or vibrating.

**tsunami**(soo • NAH • mee)—a very large ocean wave caused by
    underwater earthquakes.

**volcano**(vahl • KAY • noh)—an opening in the earth's crust
    through which lava, dust, ash, and hot gases are thrown.

# INDEX

*About the Author*

*Helen Challand earned her M.A. and Ph.D. from Northwestern University. She currently is Chair of the Science Department at National College of Education and Coordinator of Undergraduate Studies for the college's West Suburban Campus.*
   *An experienced classroom teacher and science consultant, Dr. Challand has worked on science projects for Scott Foresman and Company, Rand McNally Publishers, Harper-Row Publishers, Encyclopedia Britannica Films, Coronet Films, and Journal Films. She is associate editor for the* Young People's Science Encyclopedia *published by Childrens Press.*